Bulls with crowns within their eyes
And stately towers in their horns
Hearkened to twilight; an autumn leaf
Gave passage to kind nature...

**Vladimir Sterligov. 1948**

© Aurora Art Publishers, Leningrad, 1989
Printed in the USSR

Ф $\frac{4903020000\text{-}753}{023(01)\text{-}89}$ 34-88

ISBN 5-7300-0256-4

# Fantastic
## and
# Imaginative
# Works
## by
# Russian
# Artists

**AURORA ART PUBLISHERS**

**LENINGRAD**

Introducti
by VALERY FATEYE

Compile
by YEVGENY KOVTU
and LIUDMILA RYBAKOV

Translated from the Russia
by MARGARITA LATSINOV
and THOMAS CRAN

Designe
by YURI GAPONO
and SERGEI DYACHENK

Managing edito
MARINA GRIGORYEV

Art edito
ALEXANDER LOSHENKO

Carved decoration of the
southern facade of the
Nativity of the Virgin
Cathedral in Suzdal
(1222—25). Detail

An artist is he who puts his soul into the creation of the new, of what has never existed.

*Mikhail Prishvin*

This volume is the first-ever attempt to select and analyse those works of Russian art in which the fantasy and imagination of the artists have been most brilliantly revealed. The compilers have not restricted themselves to well-known fairy-tale illustrations and purely narrative fantastic works. They have included a large number of paintings and drawings in which the artists' imagination manifests itself not so much in the subjects depicted as in the enchanting symbolism of their imagery, in the unique plastic idiom, in their unusual colour scale reminiscent of a dream or a mirage. Thus, the book offers a wide interpretation of the fantastic: it covers not only what is unreal or non-existent but also dwells upon whimsical and unusual features in the presentation of the real phenomena.

Elements of fantasy and invention have been present in Russian art since its origin. Many of the works by Slavs from pre-historic times, such as ritualistic sculpture, relief designs on metal objects and cave drawings reflecting animistic beliefs, are wholly fantastic. Our ancestors lived in the midst of nature, were fully dependent upon it, and believed that the rustling of leaves, the splashing of water, the rolling of thunder — every sound or movement — were the signs of all-powerful forces. Anthropomorphism, the assigning of human traits to natural phenomena, provided the outlet for their lively imagination. The world surrounding the ancient Slavs, or so they perceived it, was inhabited by powerful creatures: goblins, mermaids and dryads. The sky, which could send life-giving warmth or hurl down a tempest or a blizzard, was for them the dwelling place of gods. Marked by the ingenuousness and spontaneity of primitive men's interpretation of the surrounding world, cosmogonic and totemistic myths make no clear distinction between people, animals and even plants. They feature, along with completely make-believe creatures, talking flowers, trees, birds and animals.

Mythology, with its integral and naively poetical folk idea of the world, expressed in bright metaphorical images, has always been a source for fantastic art. Folklore, and particularly fairy-tales with their miracles and wizardry, adopted such of mythology's basic elements as metamorphoses, allegories and symbols. Fairy-tales feature the imaginary beast *kitovras* (somewhat similar to the ancient Greek centaur); the mysterious, glittering Firebird, a symbol of the dream of happiness; the multi-headed serpent Gorynych the Dragon, the embodiment of evil; the hideous wizard Kashchei the Deathless; the witch Baba-Yaga; the beautiful Swan-Princess; and

pls. 5, 6
pl. 3
pl. 20

5

the people's protectors, the powerful giants Ilya Muromets, Dobrynia pl. 5
Nikitich and other mighty *bogatyrs*. Reflecting the dreams, ideals and
artistic taste of the Russian people, fairy-tales, epic songs *(bylinas)*
and legends became the thematic basis for most of the embroidery,
wood- and bone-carving, popular prints, and other folk crafts. Folklore ill. p. 11
continues to be an unfailing source of artistic inspiration.

While the fantastic themes of olden times were an expression of the
ancient Slavs' pagan beliefs, after the adoption of the Orthodox faith
via Byzantium in the tenth century the imaginary elements in Russian
art began to find their basis in Christianity (for example, the mythical
animals and birds in decorative reliefs of old Russian cathedrals elaborately
intermingled with Christian symbols). Though the iconography of religious
themes was strictly regulated, Christianity's cult of miracles and wealth
of symbols stimulated the imagination of old Russian artists. They gave
vent to their imagination by ingeniously interpreting traditional themes ill. p. 8
often stretching beyond the church canons in the process.

Ancient legends poetically combine popular beliefs and dreams of
a happy life with actual historic events. The famous tale of the invisible
city of Kitezh, miraculously saved from devastation during the invasion
of Khan Batu (1237—43) is a good example. Kitezh, so the legend
goes, disappeared under water, but a righteous man could still hear the
tolling of its bells from the shores of Lake Svetloyar. The "invisible
city", which became a symbol of the people's faith in the invincibility
of good and justice, is a traditional subject in Russian art. ill. p. 16

In the early eighteenth century, with Peter the Great's determined
introduction of Western culture, Russian art began actively employing
ancient mythology. Though Greek myths had earlier been known in Russia
through Byzantium, it was only then that mythology became an integral
part of Russian culture, and, along with Christian and folklore themes,
a major source of imaginary subject-matter. It should be noted, however,
that while this Western influence affected the culture in the cities, folk
traditions continued to hold sway in the countryside.

Gradually the influence of classical mythology, devoid of national
roots, diminished and became a feature of academic painting. Still, history
painting done in the conventional academic manner prevailed in Russian
art up through the first half of the nineteenth century.

Even the outstanding artist Alexander Ivanov in his famous canvas
*The Appearance of Christ to the People* (1837—57) was unable to
fully overcome the academic canons restricting the artist's fantasy. As far
as Ivanov's imaginative gifts are concerned, his *Biblical Studies* are perhaps ill. p. 13
of greater interest. In these visionary subjects, according to the artist
Ivan Kramskoi, "supernatural phenomena are interwoven with reality to
such a degree that when looking at the drawings one feels like a contemporary
of the distant childhood of humanity."

Those Russian masters whose interests were not connected with
historical painting, leaned towards the exact representation of reality —
usually portraiture and genre scenes. The artists painting townscapes of St.
Petersburg concentrated on the outward look of the "Northern Palmyra",
as the city was often called, trying to reproduce precisely its *grandeur*

and elegance, and stressing its strikingly consistent style. These preoccupations left little or no scope for imaginative art which was at that time practically absent from the Russian art scene.

Russian literature of that period, however, was already rich in imaginary themes not borrowed from mythology but suggested by real life. Fiodor Dostoyevsky referred to St. Petersburg as "the most fantastical city with the most fantastical history out of all the cities on the globe". This wonderful European-style city, which, at Peter the Great's will, sprang up like a miracle amidst a boggy marshland, became a major source for fantastic themes in Russian literature and later in art.

So unique was the phenomenon of St. Petersburg, so closely together did the past merge with the present on the banks of the Neva, so obviously did the city's physical appearance reveal its spiritual image and fantastic features, that many famous writers of the nineteenth century who turned to the theme of the northern capital found in it, either by intention or spontaneously, some unreal traits. Fictional subject-matter was prompted to these writers not only by the feeling of the bizarre duality of the huge planned city, erected as a challenge to nature itself, but also by the phantasmal character of the life style in this citadel of autocracy with its ruthless bureaucratic routine, by the illusoriness of reality where a person's true worth was substituted for by rank, money, property and other outward attributes.

ill. p. 18

In *The Bronze Horseman* (1833), a poem by Alexander Pushkin, the great initiator of the "golden age" of Russian literature, the equestrian statue of Peter the Great, the symbol of the empire's capital, comes down from its pedestal and chases along the embankment of the raging Neva after a "little man" who has blamed his misfortune not on the elements, but instead on the bronze horseman, the embodiment of sovereign power. In *The Nose* (1836), a story by Nikolai Gogol, the part of the face of a St. Petersburg clerk moves about on its own trying to pass off as its former master. The theme of a "double" appeared in Dostoyevsky's *St. Petersburg Stories*, which are set in a hazy atmosphere of unreality, in spite of the realism of their plots. These writers discerned an unfair and cold world full of drama and human suffering behind St. Petersburg's outer gloss and the beauty of its shimmering white nights. Fantastic themes stress the historical importance and complexity of the whole St. Petersburg period of Russian history and show how uncomfortable and lonely one felt surrounded by the stone grandeur of, as Dostoyevsky wrote, "the most abstract, the most deviously minded city on this terrestrial sphere of ours". St. Petersburg, of course, did not have a monopoly

pls. 17, 21

on imaginary subjects. The fictitious plot of *The Demon* (1841), a poem by Mikhail Lermontov, is based on a legend from the Caucasus. Its hero, the proud, suffering and powerful "exiled Demon", embodies both human and supernatural traits. Boundless Ukrainian imagination is contained in the stories by Nikolai Gogol from the series *Evenings on a Farm near Dikanka*. But still, the most significant role in prompting imaginary subjects, first in Russian literature and then in art in general, was played by St. Petersburg, with its ghostly and often absurd reality full of social contrasts, with its gap between dream and reality.

In the second half of the nineteenth century the democratically-minded *Itinerants*, as members of the Society for Circulating Art Exhibitions (1870—1923) were called, rebelled against the domination of academic routine and turned to the actual processes and social contrasts of Russian life. Uniting the most talented artists of the time, the Itinerants embodied the best traditions of the national artistic culture and made a major contribution to the formation of Russian realistic art. Though the fantastic did not play a major role in their paintings, as their aim was the objective representation of reality, it was not scorned altogether. For example, Ilya Repin, the author of the famous *Barge-Haulers on the Volga* and *The Zaporozhye Cossacks Writing a Letter to the Turkish Sultan*, employed the folk theme of a Novgorodian merchant's trip to an underwater world in his painting *Sadko in the Underwater Kingdom*.

ill. p. 17

Another indisputable achievement of the Itinerants was their bringing art back to native Russian themes. Victor Vasnetsov, said by critics to have possessed the great potential for combining the decorative and the fantastic, often turned to Russian fairy-tale and epic motifs, giving a realistic treatment to invented themes.

Nikolai Gay, whose outlook was similar to the religious and ethic teaching of Leo Tolstoy, depicted visionary scenes from the Gospels as real-life drama. His paintings combined truthfulness and sometimes even a certain down-to-earth imagery with unusual composition and outlandish colour scheme based on contrasting light and shade. Anticipating new, diverse and original art trends, fairy-tale and religious motifs received a different, somewhat more spiritual treatment in the work of Mikhail Nesterov. Innovative tendencies also grew pronounced in Valentin Serov's last works, which were based on mythological scenes.

The end of the nineteenth century, the years when the artistic principles of Nesterov and Serov were taking shape, saw a marked turn towards imaginary elements in Russian art. The time itself, filled with the anticipation of tremendous social transformations, cataclysms and the feeling of inevitable change, was to a great extent unusual and, in a way, fantastic. The turn of the century was also marked by several major scientific discoveries, such as the theory of relativity, quantum mechanics and radioactivity, which changed traditional ideas about the structure of matter and the universe. This was the time when cinema, radio, automobiles and aeroplanes, which were to introduce truly incredible changes into everyday life, were invented and being developed. These developments excited the creative imagination of artists, making them look for fresh means to express the new content. Not all of these experiments were successful, some caused heated debates, yet the attempts to determine art's future evolution were closely linked with contemporary life and its pressing spiritual concerns.

The immediate forerunner of the new art in Russia was the outstanding painter Mikhail Vrubel, whose deeply philosophic works vividly embodied the contradictions of his time. He keenly foresaw, to use the words of Alexander Blok, a poet close to him in spirit, "changes without all parallel, rebellions never known before..." It was only natural that Vrubel, a pioneer of modern art, often used fantastic subjects in his work. He borrowed his motifs from fairy-tales, *bylinas* and myths, and was able, according to his contemporaries, to see "the fantastic in the real". Vrubel's canvases, which were executed in a special, brilliantly faceted, "mosaic-like" manner, have such a way of conveying texture, volume and space, and employ such colours, that virtually every one of his subjects aroused a keen, cosmic feeling. Vrubel's original techniques alone cannot account for the secret of his profound, yet enchanting art — he lived to use Dostoyevsky's words, "through a sense of contact with other mysterious worlds". He was concerned with such fundamental issues as Good and Evil, a person's place in the Universe, the relationship of the material and the spiritual, life and death. Vrubel's works skilfully combined the imaginary and the real and were pervaded with cosmic rhythms.

A principal and recurring theme for Vrubel was that of the Demon. This preoccupation brought him both the greatest joy of creative achievement and the most distraught suffering. The futile attempts to reconcile the demonic and the human are perhaps what led to his spiritual crisis

pl. 2

pl. 1

pl. 10
ill. pp. 14—15

pls. 20—22

pl. 21

and premature death. In the image of the forlorn and tormented Demon, Vrubel tried to express the tragic feeling of his time, the romantic idea of the dual nature of the spirit and the flesh, to show the loneliness of a person isolated from society and that an ideal striven for individually can never be realized. Vrubel had a tremendous effect on the further development of art in Russia.

The neo-romantic trend, with which the appearance of paintings of fantastic subjects was closely connected, emerged at the turn of the century in St. Petersburg, the then centre of Russian artistic culture. The artists who were grouped around *The World of Art* magazine, which was published from 1899 to 1904, declared war on both conservative academic painting and the epigones of the Itinerants, the movement which had already fulfilled its task. Though in the heat of polemics the artists of this society sometimes declared the principle of "art for art's sake", they did not, in spite of their aesthetic bravado, oust social meaning from their artistic practice. The aim of their struggle was that art should not be reduced to illustrating ideas borrowed from other spheres of life cognition. They wanted to use the achievements of world culture for the renaissance of national art, and strove to provide it with a novel artistic idiom that could render the new content. Since the artists of the World of Art attached great importance to the refined professionalism and high culture of creating and interpreting paintings and graphic works, they often turned to the art of the past. Their desire to render the sentiments and premonitions that were in the air, as well as their own subjective feelings, and to reflect the enigmatic soul of the northern capital, was often assisted by the use of unreal, imaginary themes.

With its counterposing of freedom of creative imagination against philistine positivism, and with its idea that real, sensually perceived images can serve to reveal the hidden essence of phenomena and to impart to them everlasting Eternal Beauty, the World of Art was definitely close to symbolism. For example, Alexander Benois, who was the World of Art's main theoretician and who reconsidered the general concept of Russian art in terms of creating a "grand style", in his treatise *The History of Russian Art of the Nineteenth Century* (1902) had points in common with Dmitry Merezhkovsky's study *On the Reasons of the Decline and the New Trends in Modern Russian Literature* (1893), which was recognized as the first manifesto of Russian symbolism. Though the works of the World of Art artists do reflect the influence of the "decadent" images of the poets Valery Briusov, Konstantin Balmont, Fiodor Sologub and other symbolists, it was the stress on the creative, aesthetic aspect of art rather than its link with symbolism that determined the importance of this society's cultural and historical role.

The artists of the World of Art, said by critics to have opened "books for art" and "art for books", greatly raised the standing of book-design and illustration. The talent of Alexander Benois was revealed, in part, by his graphic works for books. Very much a "westerner", Benois loved the city built by Peter the Great, the person so admired by the World of Art artists, and keenly felt its soul. He was not only quite familiar with the "myth of St. Petersburg" that had taken shape in symbolist

10

THE GOOD GLUTTON AND
THE MERRY DRUNKARD.
1820s or 1830s
Engraving, tinted print.
27.7× 33 cm
The Russian Museum,
Leningrad

literature at the beginning of the century, but had himself made a substantial contribution to its formation. Noting the contradictory mixture of East and West in "Peter's city", he greatly valued St. Petersburg's orientation towards the future, and at the same time realized that the city had some ephemeral traits as a result of its isolation from the true Russia. This was reflected in Benois's illustrations to Pushkin's poem *The Bronze Horseman*, described by the painter and art critic Igor Grabar as "the glittering pearl of all Benois's work". In expressing Pushkin's interpretation of the age-old "man and society" conflict through graphic representation Benois, like the poet, actively employed fantastic elements. Remarkably, a dashing rider and a rearing horse — the images that can be traced to Russian folk traditions — became symbols of the whole of Russia and its thrust towards the future in the literature and art of the early twentieth century.

ill. p. 18

In the fine, fanciful works of Mstislav Dobuzhinsky the spiritual image of St. Petersburg is made up of two diametrically opposed emotions: admiration for the stylistic uniformity of the architecture of the past and the capital's daily face, which the artist knew intimately, and the oppressive sensation exuded by this huge man-made stone monster.

pl. 15

Dobuzhinsky's purely fantastic works brilliantly reveal his attitude towards the city as a hostile organism created by a mechanical civilization.

pl. 16

In his drawing *The Kiss*, two lovers are depicted surrounded by collapsing buildings, symbolizing the ever-victorious force of love. Only love, says the artist, can resist the attack of soulless urbanism. By their inner tension Dobuzhinsky's fantasias are reminiscent of the poems on urban themes by Emile Verhaeren and Valery Briusov. They are pervaded with an ominous atmosphere similar, for example, to that in which the action of Andrei Bely's novel *St. Petersburg* (1916) takes place.

As Victor Zamirailo's illustrations to Lermontov's poems (*Mtsyri, The Demon*, etc.) show, fantastic images are also very characteristic of his work, which exhibits a great influence of Vrubel. His frighteningly life-like *capricci* (as, in keeping with the European tradition, he termed his skilful graphic works based on imaginary subject-matter) bring to mind the symbolic paintings of Arnold Böcklin. The influence of French book illustrators, especially Gustave Doré, can also be traced in the style of his *capricci*.

pl. 17

pls. 24, 25

Thanks to his magically effective decorations and costumes to Diaghilev's famous "Russian Seasons", Leon Bakst is better known in the West than other members of the World of Art. In his painting *Terror Antiquus*, awarded the gold medal at the World Exhibition in Brussels in 1910, he employed what may be now called a cinematic eye in order to render the global character of the catastrophe. Viewed by the artist from a great height, the world is shown in panorama and includes both actual historical landmarks and fictitious details, recalling the myth of the fall of the legendary Atlantis. Though the critics saw in *Terror Antiquus* an expression of the idea of fate, universal catastrophe and Eternal Feminity in the spirit of the philosophy of Vladimir Solovyev, it is most likely that Bakst wanted to convey a concept that was closer to him, that of the eternal renovation of life. The ancient Kore's enigmatic smile stresses the transient nature of petty worldly concerns at the time of major cataclysms — a feeling common to many of Bakst's contemporaries.

pl. 12

Bakst's turn towards cosmic subjects was not accidental. The romantic outlook shared by the majority of artists of the World of Art was characterized by reflections on man's place in the universe, by seeing some supreme concealed meaning behind concrete daily phenomena and by contrasting chaotic contemporaneity with their dreams of future world harmony. For this reason a cosmic perception of reality, which usually led to the use of fantastic elements, was natural for the artists of the World of Art.

Konstantin Bogayevsky possessed a similar cosmic understanding of the world, though his manner was completely different. Drawing inspiration from his native Crimean scenery, he gave the seemingly real outlines of the mountain ranges, valleys and sea shores a generalized fantastic, "outlandish" character. The poet and artist Maximilian Voloshin, who also lived in the Crimea and was fascinated by its beauty, described Bogayevsky's highly imaginative works as dreams.

pls. 18, 19

Cosmic motifs are typical of works of Nikolai Roerich as well. His paintings combined old Russian fairy-tale and epic themes with religious symbolism and mythological Oriental subjects, and often depicted the harsh environment of the North in archaic pagan epochs, when man was part of nature. In *The Heavenly Orders*, vague symbolic images are formed by a whimsical interplay of the clouds. The immense scale in the *Red Horses* is stressed by the tiny figures of conventionally drawn horses against the background of boundless mountains stretching on to infinity. It cannot be denied, however, that Roerich's plentiful fantastic symbols, especially those going back to Oriental myths, are sometimes abundant

pl. 14
pl. 11

Alexander Ivanov.
1806—1858
WALKING UPON THE WATER. Sketch. 1850
Watercolours and white on brown paper.
26.7×39.2 cm
The Tretyakov Gallery, Moscow

in elements not directly related to painting proper, making the comprehension of the artist's general concept more difficult.

Stylization was a characteristic feature of World of Art members but it was Ivan Bilibin who made it the principal element of his art. He skilfully used his lucid ornamental technique based on linear design to recreate the favourite images of popular fantasy, framing them by purely decorative elements resembling Russian folk embroidery or carving. As with any stylization, Bilibin's manner, in spite of its originality, had considerable limitations, such as a certain rigidity of line, which made the totally imaginary subjects less convincing.

The term "retrospective dreamers", coined by the critic Sergei Makovsky to define the artists of the World of Art, best describes one of the most interesting members of the society, Konstantin Somov, though it does not apply to all aspects of his work. Recreating convincingly the atmosphere of the past, Somov's fantastic paintings show an admiration for charming details, coquettish women brightly dressed and the festivities of merry-making. Yet underlying this idyllic picture of the old life style is a sad smile, revealing his sceptical outlook. Gardens and parks with sculptures, fountains, arbours and trimmed bushes provide the setting for the action in most of his paintings, which share some traits both with the symbolistically ethereal undertones of Andrei Bely's collection of verses *Gold in Lazuli* (1904) and the affected poetry of Mikhail Kuzmin.

pls. 4, 5

pls. 7, 9

Thematically close to Somov was Victor Borisov-Musatov, who also portrayed the life style in Russian country-seats of the eighteenth century, but that is more or less where the similarity ends. Somov was a native of St. Petersburg, and his historical visions with crinolines and bosquets were, as a rule, merely refined stylizations, "masquerades", which concealed the artist's conviction that life was just a "mask of death". Representing the Moscow school of painting and deeply Russian in spirit, Borisov-Musatov perceived the past in a completely different way. Giving much less attention to the concrete signs of the epoch, he placed more value on a painting's lyrical, musical effect. Silent still figures, with the air of gentle sorrow about them, set amidst the verdure and scenery of the past, were the symbols of some ideal world. Having found refuge, as he put it, "amongst dreams and reveries", Borisov-Musatov died young, but his elegiac works had a great impact on the further development of Russian art.

pl. 30

The activity of Borisov-Musatov was connected with the appearance of a group of talented young artists in his native town of Saratov on the Volga. These artists, in particular Pavel Kuznetsov and Piotr Utkin, together with other graduates of the Moscow School of Art, formed the centre of the Blue Rose, a new artistic society. They were united by the *Golden Fleece*, a journal published by the factory-owner and amateur artist Nikolai Riabushinsky, and held their first show in 1907. Some of these artists had participated in the exhibitions of the World of Art, but, unlike the members of the latter society, gave a less concrete treatment to the prototype of the artistic image and paid increased attention to the pictorial idiom, which led them to be referred to by art critics as lyrical painters.

The artists of the Blue Rose had more clearly revealed their ties with symbolism; they impressionistically combined musical motifs with vivid and often fantastically ephemeral range of colours. In connection with the Blue Rose, it is appropriate to recall a critic's opinion that the art of St. Petersburg was dominated by drawing, while Moscow was "the capital of colour". In the charming canvases of its representatives,

the outlines of earthly objects are mollified, the colours are pale and soft, the sky almost melts into the earth, everything becomes dissolved in the colourful lyrical medium. These artists were close in spirit to the younger symbolist generation of "theurgist" poets — Alexander Blok, Andrei Bely and Viacheslav Ivanov — with their tendency *a realibus ad realiora* (from the outward to the inward and supreme) and the desire to overcome the decadence of their forerunners. The members of the Blue Rose also strove to abandon the fatalistic individualism common to some sceptical "westerners" of the World of Art, and move on to highly sublime and invigorating art, where man would be connected with nature by the "intimate tie of existence". No longer satisfied with the excessive bookishness and rationalistic intellectuality of the works done by the World of Art members, the painters of the new society leaned towards an exhalted expression of emotions through purely painterly means. It is no coincidence that some artists of the Blue Rose were fascinated with deliberate decorative exquisiteness.

An ingenuous perception of the world, dreaminess and a sincere lyricism distinguished the best masters of the Blue Rose. These traits gave a fantastic flavour to almost all of their works. Pavel Kuznetsov, in addition to all this, possessed an extremely fine feeling for colour, which was particularly apparent in his paintings of Kirghizia. Piotr Utkin's early works were marked by a deep understanding of nature, soft and noble tonality and melancholy contemplation.

Martiros Saryan, a prominent Armenian artist who studied in Moscow and was inseparably linked with Russian artistic culture, was also a member of the Blue Rose. In the early 1900s Saryan, endowed with an original perception of reality, painted fairy-tale and other imaginary themes. Such of his early works as *The Poet* and *The Panthers,* where reality and fantasy are conjoined, as in ancient mythology or folklore, and human and animal features blur, are remarkable for their riot of colour and combination of Russian artistic tradition with bright Oriental imagery. Saryan perceived nature with a poetic integrity; his trees blaze like flames lit at some cosmic festival for the wholeness of being.

pls. 31, 32, 34

pl. 33

pl. 35

15

The Lithuanian Mikalojus Čiurlionis, another artist of lyrical talent, had an affinity with the Russian innovators, and, after moving to St. Petersburg in 1909, took part in their exhibitions. The special charm of his colourful reveries comes from his talent as both an artist and a composer. In the "translucent" musical images and in the rhythm of his compositions, Čiurlionis strove to create some ideal synthesis of a person's inner world, express the harmony of existence and evoke the feeling of eternity. At the same time, he possessed a cordial and sensitive attitude towards the world; his poetic fantasias, often built around the vertical axes, stress elevated aspirations, and turn one's thoughts to the ties between people and heavens. The works by Čiurlionis had a profound impact on all Russian artists who painted cosmic scenes.

Also close to symbolism at the beginning of his career was Kuzma Petrov-Vodkin, another artist from the Volga region and one of the younger generation of the World of Art group. He, however, worked in a manner different from that of the "lyrical artists". He did not dissolve the form in the "soothing horror of indefiniteness", as did, in his mind, the artists of the Blue Rose. Relying on Old Russian icon painting, he worked out his authentic monumental style, which organically incorporated national tradition and modern quests. A student of Anton Ažbe in Munich, Petrov-Vodkin was also influenced by Pierre Puvis de Chavannes and Jules Bastien-Lepage. His greatest achievements, however, are connected with his own discoveries in painting. Typifying this artist

**Ivan Bilibin.** 1876—1942
KITEZH TRANSFORMED.
Stage-set design for the opera *The Tale of the Invisible City of Kitezh and the Maiden Fevronia* by N. Rimsky-Korsakov. 1929
Lead pencil, watercolours, gold and silver on paper pasted on cardboard.
54.3×73.2 cm
The Russian Museum, Leningrad

**Ilya Repin.** 1844—1930
SADKO IN THE UNDERWATER KINGDOM. 1876
Oil on canvas.
322.5×230 cm
The Russian Museum, Leningrad

pl. 13
pl. 73

are bright local colour, rhythmical expressiveness, two-dimensional representation combined with spatial constructions on many planes, and the impression of an action being a frozen fragment of a dream. Later he began employing spherical perspective and achieved a global view of reality by bringing together several points of vision.

The domination in symbolist literature of abstract philosophical allegories that were centred on ideas rather than words led to the appearance of opposing trends, futurism and acmeism. Similarly, the World of Art and the Blue Rose gave way to Russian avant-garde artists who were possessed with the idea of innovation. Headed by Mikhail Larionov, they proclaimed a complete revision of the old artistic traditions and firmly maintained a purely structural and plastic perception of the world. This was a period of "the tempest and the fury", the beginning of a true revolution in art, and fantastic interpretation of reality was typical of the works of most of these avant-garde artists.

The leaders of the future main trends of Russian avant-garde art, such as Mikhail Larionov, Kasimir Malevich, Vladimir Tatlin, Wassily Kandinsky and others, were revealed as early as 1910 at the exhibitions of the Jack of Diamonds and Union of the Young. Having studied and assimilated the latest Western achievements of post-impressionism, fauvism, cubism and so on, they left them behind to go still further. Inspired by the quest for the new, previously unheard-of, as well as by the spirit of competition for priority of artistic revelations, these artists, since they represented differing trends, often clashed. As they issued new manifestoes, formed new groupings and organized new exhibitions, a unique, unprecedented and very contradictory phenomenon emerged, which was to become famous as the Russian avant-garde of the early twentieth century. Its main tendencies were shaped before the First World War, and it later developed along already chosen paths. Russian art, having come a long and difficult way in a short period of time, became notable in the world artistic development.

Nearly each of the avant-garde artists mentioned in this book is a unique master with an original perception of the world and his individual plastic pattern of representing it. The global vision inherent in transitional epochs, bold aspirations towards the future, destruction of the borderline between objective reality and the subjective sensations of an artist who transforms the world, artistic patterns of a paradoxical character breaking established traditions, and the feeling that time can be "overcome" and expressed via space — these are the features of the world outlook shared by the avant-garde artists which promoted the penetration of fantastic elements into their works. Often these innovative artists portrayed the intangible as visible and vice versa: in some of their canvases real objects and figures acquire fantastical appearance. The pulling together of phenomena relating to different temporal strata and the combining of unreal structural forms with elements of reality transformed by imagination were other commonly employed devices. Sometimes the subjective treatment of the world resulted in a completely non-objective representation.

Dostoyevsky's observation that it is common for Russian people to go to extremes in everything is often referred to by foreign art historians

Alexander Benois.
1870—1960
Frontispiece for
*The Bronze Horseman*
by A. Pushkin. 1905
Watercolours and white.
29×22 cm
The All-Union Pushkin
Museum, Leningrad

when explaining the radical character of Russian avant-garde art. Though rather apt, this reference is one-sided. Russian avant-garde art was a result of a whole complex of social, cultural and historical factors. It was, however, not the idea of destroying form and tradition that motivated the best representatives of this trend, but rather the belief that the creative force of their art could change the world. Some art critics had an overriding tendency to stress merely the formalistic and utilitarian leanings in Russian avant-garde painting, largely ignoring the other aspects of this movement, that are no less essential and typically national — the spiritual and creative ones. Notwithstanding their extremes and defiance, a striving took shape in the quests of Russian artists towards the synthesis of the intuitive and analytic approaches; towards the dialectic integrity of form and content, fantasy and reality; towards the treatment of man as an integral part of nature and the universe — all of which would have an impact later on.

At a certain stage, the activity of the avant-garde artists, almost all of whom were members of the Union of the Young, was closely connected with the poets of a similar literary society, Hylaea. The latter were futurists, or, as they termed themselves, *budetliane,* coining a new word from a Slavic root in order to emphasize their independence from Italian futurism, which was dominated by mechanical, antihuman traits. The artists close to futurism were united with these poets by a common antiphilistine orientation and a rebellious denial of bourgeois culture, their activity sometimes taking the radical forms of extreme nihilism and self-advertisement. The banner of futurism attracted people of various views and degrees of talent, yet in creative terms they were all brought together by the desire to renew the artistic and poetic idiom, and by an inclination towards materially feasible images and to increasing their immediate expressiveness. Many of the members of the union were both artists and poets. In their lithographed books of verses, the text, usually hand-written, and the design were equal and formed a unity. Among the avant-garde artists illustrating the books of the futurists were Larionov, Malevich, Tatlin, Goncharova, Filonov, Rozanova and Guro. These artists were sometimes called cubofuturists — an erroneous label primarily because their evolution was especially marked by an abandonment of cubism and its concern for geometric forms, by the adherence to folk art and the heritage of Old Russian culture and by the strong influence of Oriental art.

pl. 42
ill. p. 23

As most members of this movement agreed, the main originator of new ideas was the poet Velimir Khlebnikov. Along with Vladimir Mayakovsky, this utopian dreamer and daring innovator played a major role in carrying out the main task of futurism — to enhance the importance of a "self-contained" word, the primary cell of a literary image, and give it back its initial pertinence and vigour. On top of that, being endowed with a superb feeling for language, Khlebnikov tried to revitalize the semantic content of the word's basic constituents, i.e., its sounds. He hoped, with the help of these "word seeds", to recreate a universal "celestial" (or "transsense") vernacular that would go deeper than concepts expressed by words, and penetrate into the very essence of objects and

**Kuzma Petrov-Vodkin.**
1878—1930
ON THE SHORE. 1908
Oil on canvas.
128×159 cm
The Russian Museum,
Leningrad

phenomena. In this respect his method was similar to the efforts by Pavel Filonov, who traced a likeness between the microstructures of an image and the "atoms" of the organic world.

Khlebnikov's fanciful hypotheses stirred the imagination of poets and artists alike. He did not differentiate between dream and reality in his work, his bold utopian schemes inspiring a search for a universal outlook, a global view of man's interrelations with civilization and nature. Paying special attention to the investigation into the problem of time, Khlebnikov managed to freely join images and ideas from differing cultures and epochs, bridging the gap between the pagan simplicity of a countryside idyll and the dream of the future's scientific and technological achievements. He was driven by the idea of creating a modern myth that would be a universal and cosmogonic synthesis organically combining the perception of reality peculiar to natural philosophy with the outlook of a man of the twentieth century — a man enriched with the knowledge of science and technology but at the same time not overwhelmed by it or impaired by rationalism. Khlebnikov's future-oriented poetic "cosmogony" stimulated artists who were also seeking to incarnate the twentieth century's more complicated ideas of the world in their imagery.

The most active of the artists of this union was Mikhail Larionov, a tireless experimenter who exerted considerable influence on Russian pre-revolutionary art. Described by the French poet Guillaume Apollinaire as an artist of "extremely strong individuality", Larionov often changed, in search of the new, the direction of his quest. From impressionism *à la* Borisov-Musatov he went to primitivism and later evolved the so-called rayonism, which Guillaume Apollinaire considered an artistic contribution of European significance. Since he consistently struggled for a national basis in painting, his most independent works can be traced to the traditions of folk art. He sought to free art from rationalist traits and render the form as if perceived by a naive consciousness. His view of the world, like that of a man unaffected by civilization, brings him close to literary acmeism and the patriarchal mythologyzing of Khlebnikov.

In his painting *Venus* Larionov achieves great expressiveness by boldly simplifying form and using inscriptions as a decorative element. Also interesting is the technique shown in his improvisations based on Oriental fairy-tales, as well as the fanciful treatment of colour in the lithographs for the book *Lipstick* by Alexei Kruchenykh, a radical futurist poet.

pl. 41

pl. 38

pl. 42

Natalia Goncharova, who, according to Marina Tsvetayeva, the artist's counterpart in poetry, was "wholly a direct assertion of life", explicitly intertwined traditions and innovation in her works. Various in manner, they were often inspired by the latest discoveries of the inventive Larionov, yet, in spite of their changing style and freedom in choice of expressive means, they were invariably stamped with her powerful temperament and distinct individuality. She managed to combine colour and linear decorativeness with an expressive imagery. The treatment of visionary subjects in Goncharova's *Mystic Images of War* series shows the typical traits of her style. Depicted against the background of modern urban structures, the apocalyptic "iron birds" are rhythmically in tune with the images of flying angels and also full of the futurist dynamism of the time when the first aeroplanes appeared. She freely used the traditions of Old Russian icon and mural painting, as well as those of manuscript illumination. Marina Tsvetayeva said that the activity of Goncharova stands at "the meeting point of West and East, Past and Future, people and an individual, labour and talent". Calling her "a great Russian artist", Apollinaire stressed the dynamism of Goncharova's compositions, saying that "movement in her art is a dance made rhythmical by enthusiasm."

pls. 48, 50

Wassily Kandinsky, the founder of abstract painting, was another major figure in the Russian avant-garde. In his early works he was still depicting the objective world, although even then he viewed reality through the prism of his imagination. *St. George the Warrior on Horseback* is interesting for the unusual, almost, fairy-tale interpretation that the future "non-objectivist" painter gave to this popular theme in Russian art. Another of his paintings, *Moonlit Night*, shows that the nature of his talent was closer to the World of Art; it was not without reason that his teaching of pure "spiritual harmony" in painting was considered by some artists as too "literary".

pl. 37

pl. 36

**Olga Rozanova.**
1886—1918
BATTLE IN THE
CITY.
Illustration for the book
*War* by A. Kruchenykh.
1916
Linocut. 27.5×22 cm
The Russian Museum,
Leningrad

pl. 51

pl. 52

Marc Chagall was completely led by his imagination. Very early in his career he created his own, easily recognizable world of flights and reveries — a dreamlike and mischievous world of a child who believes in miracles. Wide-ranging colour improvisation and the particular ethnographic details of the life of provincial Jewish communities were also peculiar to this world. In spite of the repetitious use of subjects and manner in the future, this "visionary" artist always found new expressive interpretations with which to charm his viewer.

The majority of the artists mentioned here worked both before and after the revolution of 1917, yet their fates were not the same. Some (many of the World of Art members, Kandinsky, Chagall) soon found themselves abroad. Losing, along with their homeland, the national roots that had fed their work, these artists were doomed from then on to repeat what had already been achieved. Others (Petrov-Vodkin, Tatlin, Kuznetsov, Filonov) welcomed the revolution, and made its thrust towards the future, towards the new and unprecedented, a powerful stimulus for the all-round development of their creative fantasy.

For Pavel Filonov the choice was easy. Being "a proletarian artist", as he called himself, after the revolution he continued with redoubled energy the work he had already begun for the creation of art of a new epoch. His art shows a striking similarity with the poetry of Khlebnikov. Every bit as bold and devoted an innovator, he managed to achieve supreme expressiveness and emotional power in his paintings, thanks to a special micro-treatment of the various parts and structures of the canvas. The imaginative non-objective primary elements, functioning in a way like Khlebnikov's "word seeds", gained independent artistic meaning in the overall scheme, and acted as living "monads" growing to form figurative images.

Filonov considered the "invention of forms" in the process of work, and the synthesis of the intuitive and the thought-out when "making" a painting, an achievement of his "analytical method". He was the first artist to introduce a recreation of the invisible biological processes of growth and movement into painting, which he achieved by building up non-objective "atoms" to reveal natural, living forms.

Though going far beyond Vrubel in the illusory treatment of reality, Filonov's carefully elaborated structures can be partly traced back to the influence of that artist's "crystalline" method.

Each of Filonov's paintings is a pregnant embodiment of many layers of associations, interrelations and "meaningful forms". Their play of fantasy, and varied and whimsical reflection of the world bring the works of Hieronymus Bosch and Peter Brueghel to mind; but Filonov's paintings have also a "magical" touch peculiar to primitive art. Some of his "hermetic" paintings leave an oppressive sensation because of their absence of harmony, and their juxtaposition of the "vivisectional" naturalism of disjointed fragments with an elaborate conception of the whole design. In the works where analysis dominated synthesis, where the artist failed to beautify the inert material by the force of his inspiration; in them he was closer, to continue the literary comparison, to the infinitely fragmentary world of the "consciousness panoramas" of Andrei Bely's later prose than to Khlebnikov's writing. Filonov's works became much integral when living natural images prevailed in his "atoms", rather than those that were cold and angular, or anatomically dissected. The artist's major achievement was his emphasis on both form and content, his centering on natural structures and processes instead of abstract and rational modules. Filonov, a great, purely Russian phenomenon in art, was, in terms of imaginative power, undoubtedly one of the leading artists of his time. He had many disciples, and the works by Tatyana Glebova, for example, are interesting for the way she transformed his unique style.

Another major figure in art during the period of the revolution was Vladimir Tatlin, whose imagination was directed primarily at exposing the inner structure of things, and showing the unity of their form and material. Being inclined to the study of the structural laws of organic

pls. 62, 63

Pavel Basmanov.
Born 1906
A STROLL WITH THE CHILDREN. 1933
Watercolours.
16.3 × 20 cm
Private collection, Leningrad

pls. 64—66

24

nature, his vision of the world was broader than merely the utilitarian and industrial understanding of constructivism usually associated with his name. Tatlin's bionic engineering made itself felt even in his costume sketches for the popular drama *Tsar Maxemyan and His Unruly Son Adolfa*. In addition to the famous design of a tower, a monument to the Third International, his flying machine *Letatlin* was of interest. Designed in 1932, it was a bionic utopia relying on the biological principles of birds' flight rather than mechanical computation.

pls. 54, 55

Prominent among the Russian avant-garde artists, especially after Larionov left in 1914 to execute decorations for Diaghilev's ballets abroad, was Kasimir Malevich. During the Soviet times he continued working out the laws of suprematism, a trend that he had invented before the revolution. His entire life was endless experiments: after painting works with semi-fantastic colour schemes, already showing the influence of cubism, he went on to create a realm where objects and people were turned into dynamic geometric forms. Still later, led by a thirst for innovation, he completely abandoned natural shapes and subordinated his gift to the

pls. 57, 58, 67

rigid formula of the "pure painterly plastics" of suprematism. By ousting the "gravitation of terrestrial objects" from painting and juxtaposing instead various colour and surface structures, he thought he would introduce a new universal space and a sense of motion different from that achieved by the futurists. In the late 1920s Malevich returned to figurative means of expression without abandoning his suprematist principles.

The work by Vladimir Sterligov, a disciple of Malevich, is also of interest. Strongly influenced in his early works by suprematism, he later departed from the linear approach expounded by his teacher and, relying on the curvilinear concept of the Universe, elaborated more complex and multi-dimensional imaginary forms.

The scientific study of colour was continued after the revolution by Mikhail Matiushin. His theory of "expanded vision" made it possible to greatly enhance the impact of colour on the viewer. Matiushin's works reproduced here, especially the watercolour *On the Death of Yelena Guro,* with its pulsating cosmic rhythms, confirm the value of this artist's theoretical and practical searchings. In the work by his disciple Maria Ender, *Experiment on a New Spatial Measure,* the depth and three-dimensional character of space are brilliantly conveyed by the rhythmically organized blots of light and dark saturated colour.

"Classic" constructivism was transformed into a specifically fantastic overload of technical details and the poetic treatment of civilization's industrial achievements in some paintings by Kliment Redko. Yet his especially attractive works are those extremely emotional, mirage-like, charming, romantic landscapes of the Russian North. According to André Salmon, who in 1929 published a monograph in Paris about Redko, "he treated the midnight sun in the same way as a flashlight" and enlivened the snow-covered polar expanses by depicting on them "gentle beasts and mysterious birds" of exaggerated dimensions. These northern landscapes by Redko are characterized by a feeling of unity with nature and a cosmic view of reality.

Though of a completely different sort, a cosmic outlook was also peculiar to a gifted friend of the young Redko, Vasily Chekrygin. Chekrygin who died tragically at the age of twenty five, with the direction of development of his unique talent still unclear, was, according to many, a potential genius. When just sixteen he illustrated Mayakovsky's book of verses *Me!* These illustrations, revealing the influence of icon painting, are drawn with a strikingly fluent line. Leaving behind an interest in the newest Western trends, though not breaking with the tradition of great realist art, Chekrygin began a quest for realism of a new kind, marked by cosmic undertones, and a stunning unity of elevated, dramatic content and innovative form. The artist left a great number of sketches for some gigantic, yet not quite fully shaped projects. The emotional and semi-fantastic world of these drawings testifies to an integrity of talent unusual for our time, and to the artist's great creative force and wealth of imagination. The figures that emerge from a glittering chiaroscuro are depicted at dramatic moments of extreme universal importance, and, despite their flickering mysteriousness and transparency, have a palpable plasticity, tragic intensity and the dynamism of creative action.

pl. 60

pls. 59, 61

pl. 43

pl. 39

pl. 75

pl. 71

pl. 70
pl. 72

Chekrygin's spiritual fervour was fed by the ideas of the utopian philosopher Nikolai Fiodorov (1828—1903), who showed in his typically Russian teaching that people should join their efforts like brothers in "common cause" to get control over nature. It was, incidentally, Fiodorov's ideas on the exploration of space as a necessary stage in human evolution towards future brotherhood, though then seemingly impossible, that inspired Konstantin Tsiolkovsky to design the space rocket. Chekrygin's understanding of the world as a spiritualized cosmos and of creative activity as a cause shared by the whole of mankind, both of which he got from Fiodorov, made him similar to Mikhail Prishvin, Nikolai Zabolotsky, Andrei Platonov and other writers and poets of his time.

pls. 26, 27

Oskar Klever, a theatre artist who devoted much time to illustrating the fairy-tales by Hans Christian Andersen, also produced fascinating "musical" compositions in watercolour with multiple worlds vanishing in the distance.

A unique, romantic realm was created in the works by another theatre artist, Alexander Tyshler. Though having his own scenic perception of the world, his boundless imagination and mysterious vibration of brushwork bear a similarity to Chagall's. For Tyshler, life was a fancy-dress ball or a brightly decorated stage full of wonderful metamorphoses where the seemingly impossible became quite convincing and natural. The artist stuck to one set of imaginary motifs, most often these were slender

pl. 53

female figures carrying bizarre still-life arrangements or even architectural designs on their heads. Tyshler's magical and extremely imaginative art had a great influence on modern stage-set designers.

The gouache paintings by Vera Yermolayeva deserve special mention, though she is mostly known for her illustrations of the books by Daniil Kharms, Nikolai Zabolotsky, Alexander Vvedensky and other poets of the "society of real art" (oberiuty) who developed Khlebnikov's ideas in children's literature in the 1920s and '30s. Her graphic works display

pls. 68, 69

a soft, fluid manner and eloquent understatements giving their outwardly simple themes a charm of mystery and depth. Looking as if submerged in a subtle haze, her vague yet convincing figures populate some fantastic world having its own laws of time and space. They have a disturbing quality, and arouse philosophic musings and a feeling of being introduced to the mysteries of the Universe. This is most vividly sensed in the gouache painting *Lucretius Pointing at the Sun*, which conveys the cosmogonic character of

pl. 74

the teaching of this famous Roman philosopher.

Pavel Basmanov is an artist who managed to achieve a happy combi-

ill. p. 25

pl. 78

nation of innovation and the deep-rooted traditions of Russian art. His festively bright watercolours with a fine rhythmical balance have nothing strident or discordant about them. People of slightly elongated proportions, devoid of any concrete features, appear against a background of the vast steppe producing the impression of an unrealized dream, of an ideal or of a memory of distant childhood. Making skilful use of purely plastic means, he miraculously transformed life episodes of little importance into symbols of beauty and universal harmony, of man's inseparable link with the earth and heavens. His watercolours are full of heart-felt lyricism, a love for life and his native scenery, they breathe a sense of eternity.

The emotional realm of his paintings is created primarily by a harmony of colour, whose purity of tone suggests a comparison with the frescoes by Dionysius and the paintings by Pavel Kuznetsov; other aspects of his style show the influence of Malevich. Despite the rather narrow scope of his themes, Basmanov is one of the few artists of his generation who expressed the Russian spiritual ideal of beauty — a task that only an artist endowed with a pure soul, intuition and rich imagination could cope with.

Naturally, the circle of artists whose work shows a wide use of fantasy, could be considerably enlarged, since the best paintings and drawings by Russian masters are marked, as a rule, by the wealth of imagination, variety and boldness of artistic solutions, as well as by profound philosophical concepts, prevailing among which is the idea of the cosmic unity of man and nature, vital in our days.

The works of Russian artists based on imaginary themes are nowadays attracting greater attention because of their intense connection with reality, the link they establish between the past and the present and, of course, because of their bold insights into the future. Now that space, the planetary unity of all living beings and universal cosmic rhythms have become concepts impinging on us all rather than an unusual perception shared by a few highly intuitive individuals, many paintings, previously viewed as unreal fantasies or dreams, have come to be perceived differently. Especially attractive in these bright images brimming over with imagination is the comprehension of a man as a microcosm of the universe, and the feeling of the beauty and mystery of world as an organic whole. Although sometimes naive in terms of philosophy and moot in terms of aesthetics, these attempts by artists to penetrate cosmic mysteries help us to better visualize the scope of human possibilities and direct our activity towards implementing the beautiful dream of mankind's unity and the harmony of man with nature and the cosmos.

*VALERY FATEYEV*

1  **Nikolai Gay. 1831—1894**
CALVARY. 1893
Oil on canvas. 222.4× 191 cm
The Tretyakov Gallery, Moscow

2  **Victor Vasnetsov. 1848—1926**
THREE PRINCESSES. 1884
Oil on canvas. 173× 295 cm
Museum of Russian Art, Kiev

3  **Victor Vasnetsov. 1848—1926**
KASHCHEI THE DEATHLESS
Oil on canvas. 196× 306 cm
The V. Vasnetsov Memorial Museum, Moscow

4  **Ivan Bilibin. 1876—1942**
"OUR TSAREVICH, MUCH AMAZED,
AT A SPACIOUS CITY GAZED..."
Illustration for *The Tale of Tsar Saltan*
by A. Pushkin. 1905
Watercolours and tempera. 30× 22.5 cm
The Russian Museum, Leningrad

2

3

4

6

5  **Ivan Bilibin.** 1876—1942
DOBRYNIA NIKITICH FREEING
ZABAVA PUTIATICHNA FROM
GORYNYCH THE DRAGON. 1941
Watercolours. 45.5×34.5 cm
The Russian Museum, Leningrad

6  **Konstantin Somov.** 1869—1939
Cover for the book of verses *The Firebird*
by K. Balmont. 1923
Watercolours and gouache. 21×17 cm
The Tretyakov Gallery, Moscow

9

**7 Konstantin Somov.** 1869—1939
FIREWORKS. 1922
Oil on canvas. 60×90 cm
The I. Brodsky Memorial Museum,
Leningrad

**8 Konstantin Somov.** 1869—1939
WIZARDRY. 1898(?)
Gouache, white, lead pencil and bronze.
49.5×34.1 cm
The Russian Museum, Leningrad

**9 Konstantin Somov.** 1869—1939
ITALIAN COMEDY. 1914
Watercolours and gouache. 18.5×22 cm
The Picture Gallery of Armenia, Yerevan

11

10  **Mikhail Nesterov.** 1862—1942
PRINCESS. 1887
Oil on canvas. 81×46 cm
Private collection, Moscow

11  **Nikolai Roerich.** 1874—1947
RED HORSES. 1925
Tempera on cardboard. 73×100.5 cm
Art Museum, Gorky

13

**12 Leon Bakst.** 1866—1924
TERROR ANTIQUUS. 1908
Oil on canvas. 250×270 cm
The Russian Museum, Leningrad

**13 Kuzma Petrov-Vodkin.** 1878—1939
DREAM. 1911
Oil on canvas. 161×187 cm
The Russian Museum, Leningrad

**14 Nikolai Roerich.** 1874—1947
THE HEAVENLY ORDERS. 1915
Tempera on cardboard. 75×97.5 cm
The Russian Museum, Leningrad

**15 Mstislav Dobuzhinsky.** 1875—1957
CITY DREAMS. STILLNESS. 1918
Black chalk and charcoal. 82×59.5 cm
The Russian Museum, Leningrad

**16 Mstislav Dobuzhinsky.** 1875—1957
THE KISS. 1916
Sauce-crayon and sanguine on primed
plywood. 109×77.7 cm
The Russian Museum, Leningrad

15

17

17 **Victor Zamirailo.** 1868—1939
THE DEMON
Watercolours and ink. 30.8×22.5 cm
The Russian Museum, Leningrad

18 **Konstantin Bogayevsky.** 1872—1943
FANTASTIC LANDSCAPE
WITH THE SUN. 1911
Tempera and gouache. 78×67.4 cm
The Russian Museum, Leningrad

1

19

**19  Konstantin Bogayevsky.** 1872—1943
LANDSCAPE
Watercolours. 25.8×36.1 cm
The Russian Museum, Leningrad

**20  Mikhail Vrubel.** 1856—1910
THE SWAN-PRINCESS. Sketch. 1900
Oil on panel. 23×18.9 cm
The Russian Museum, Leningrad

22

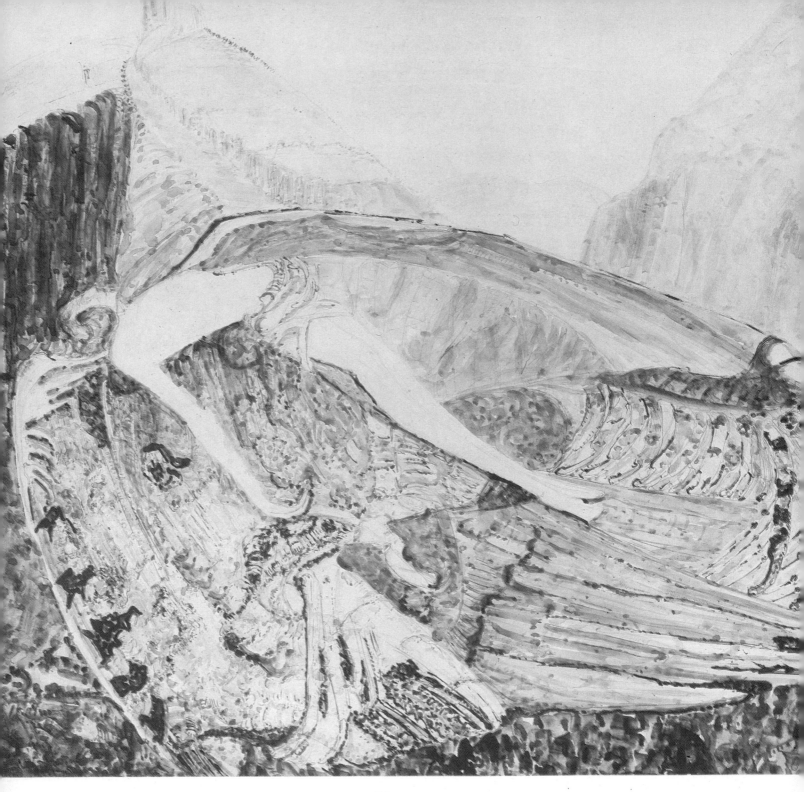

23

**23   Vasily Denisov.** 1862—1920
**THE DEMON PROSTRATED.**
**ON THE DEATH OF M. VRUBEL.** 1910
Watercolours and lead pencil. 48×56.6 cm
The Russian Museum, Leningrad

24

**24 Victor Zamirailo.** 1868—1939
NIGHT. 1908
Watercolours and white on paper pasted on
cardboard. 29.5×29.2 cm
The Russian Museum, Leningrad

25

**25   Victor Zamirailo.** 1868—1939
WITCH. 1910
Watercolours, lead pencil and white.
31.4× 32 cm
The Russian Museum, Leningrad

**26   Oskar Klever.** 1887—1975
SONATA. PART I. 1922. Detail
Watercolours. 69.5× 60 cm
Private collection, Leningrad

27

**27   Oskar Klever.** 1887—1975
SONATA: ETERNAL TRANSFORMATION
OF THE PRIMORDIAL POSSIBILITIES
(ALLEGRO MOLTO). PART I.
1935, finished in 1964
Watercolours. 60×69.5 cm
Private collection, Leningrad

28

**28 Mikalojus Čiurlionis.** 1875—1911
THE SACRIFICE. 1909
Tempera on cardboard. 47,5×50.5 cm
The Russian Museum, Leningrad

29

29   **Mikalojus Čiurlionis.** 1875—1911
PRELUDE
Watercolours, lead pencil and white.
63.3×73 cm
The Russian Museum, Leningrad

30   **Victor Borisov-Musatov.** 1870—1905
ENCOUNTER AT A COLUMN
Watercolours, pen and ink. 17.8×12.2 cm
The Russian Museum, Leningrad

31

**31  Pavel Kuznetsov.** 1878—1968
A sketch of the curtain for the ballet
*The Firebird* by I. Stravinsky. 1923
Watercolours. 46×57 cm
The Russian Museum, Leningrad

**32  Pavel Kuznetsov.** 1878—1968
FORTUNE-TELLING. 1908. Detail
Oil on canvas. 72×75.5 cm
The Russian Museum, Leningrad

34

33  **Piotr Utkin.** 1877—1934
AT THE SEA. 1910. Detail
Watercolours, gouache and white.
48.5×42.7 cm
The Russian Museum, Leningrad

34  **Pavel Kuznetsov.** 1878—1968
MIRAGE IN A STEPPE. 1912
Tempera on canvas. 95×103 cm
The Tretyakov Gallery, Moscow

35  **Martiros Saryan.** 1880—1972
THE PANTHERS. 1907
Tempera and oil on canvas. 35.5×51 cm
The Picture Gallery of Armenia, Yerevan

36

**36  Wassily Kandinsky.** 1866—1944
MOONLIT NIGHT. 1907
Wood engraving and watercolours.
20.8×18.6 cm
The Tretyakov Gallery, Moscow

**37  Wassily Kandinsky.** 1866—1944
ST. GEORGE THE WARRIOR
ON HORSEBACK
Oil on cardboard. 61.4×91 cm
The Tretyakov Gallery, Moscow

**38  Mikhail Larionov.** 1881—1964
ORIENTAL MOTIF. 1898
Gouache, ink and bronze. 15.5×23.6 cm
The Russian Museum, Leningrad

37

40

39  **Maria Ender.** 1897—1942
EXPERIMENT ON A NEW
SPATIAL MEASURE. 1920. Detail
Oil on canvas. 65.6×65.6 cm
The Russian Museum, Leningrad

40  **Mikhail Matiushin.** 1861—1934
THE FLOWER OF A MAN. 1918
Watercolours and coloured ink. 26×23 cm
The Russian Museum, Leningrad

42

41

**41 Mikhail Larionov.** 1881—1964
VENUS. 1912
Oil on canvas. 68×85.5 cm
The Russian Museum, Leningrad

**42 Mikhail Larionov.** 1881—1964
PALM-TREE. Illustration for the book
*Lipstick* by A. Kruchenykh. 1913
Lithograph, tinted print. 10.5×7.8 cm
The Russian Museum, Leningrad

43

**43 Mikhail Matiushin.** 1861—1934
ON THE DEATH OF YELENA GURO. 1918
Watercolours. 38.4×27 cm
The Russian Museum, Leningrad

**44 Yelena Guro.** 1877—1913
SCANDINAVIAN PRINCESS. 1910. Detail
Oil on canvas. 70×70 cm
The Russian Museum, Leningrad

**45** Vladimir Kozlinsky. 1888—1967
"SPANISH" FLU. 1919
Linocut. 29×21.3 cm
The Russian Museum, Leningrad

**46** Pavel Mansurov. 1896—1985
MIRAGE. 1918
Black watercolour. 18.5×13.1 cm
The Russian Museum, Leningrad

47

**47 Lev Bruni.** 1894—1948
RAINBOW. 1915
Oil on canvas. 67×67 cm
The Russian Museum, Leningrad

**48 Natalia Goncharova.** 1881—1962
THE DOOMED CITY.
From the *Mystic Images of War* series. 1914
Lithograph. 31×23.5 cm
The Russian Museum, Leningrad

**49  Lev Bruni.** 1894—1948
"MISTAKE OF THE DEATH".
Based on the poem of the same
title by V. Khlebnikov
Tempera. 52×60 cm
The Russian Museum, Leningrad

49

50

50 Natalia Goncharova. 1881—1962
ANGELS AND AEROPLANES. From the
*Mystic Images of War* series. 1914
Lithograph. 30.7×22.6 cm
The Russian Museum, Leningrad

51

**51 Marc Chagall.** 1887—1985
STROLL. 1917
Oil on canvas. 170×163.3 cm
The Russian Museum, Leningrad

52

52  **Marc Chagall.** 1887—1985
HOUSE ON THE OUTSKIRTS. 1914
Pen and ink. 14×15.1 cm
The Russian Museum, Leningrad

53

**53  Alexander Tyshler.** 1898—1980
SEMI-NUDE. From the *Couches with Candles* series. 1977
Oil on canvas. 70×70 cm
Private collection, Moscow

КУМЕРСКАЯ                    ВЕНЕРА

4/XI 11г.

ВИНЕРИН ЗАДИРЩИК

55

**54 Vladimir Tatlin.** 1885—1953
"KUMERIAN VENUS". A sketch for the folk drama *Tsar Maxemyan and His Unruly Son Adolfa.* 1911
Lead pencil and watercolours. 24×16.7 cm
The Russian Museum, Leningrad

**55 Vladimir Tatlin.** 1885—1953
"VENUS'S TEASE". A sketch for the folk drama *Tsar Maxemyan and His Unruly Son Adolfa.* 1911
Lead pencil and watercolours. 24×16.7 cm
The Russian Museum, Leningrad

56

**56  Olga Rozanova.** 1886—1918
DANCERS ON THE STAGE.
Illustration for the book *The Duck's Nest
of Obscene Words* by A. Kruchenykh. 1913
Lithograph, tinted print. 10.7×16.5 cm
The Russian Museum, Leningrad

**57  Kasimir Malevich.** 1878—1935
PEASANT. 1928(?)
Oil on canvas. 129×98.5 cm
The Russian Museum, Leningrad

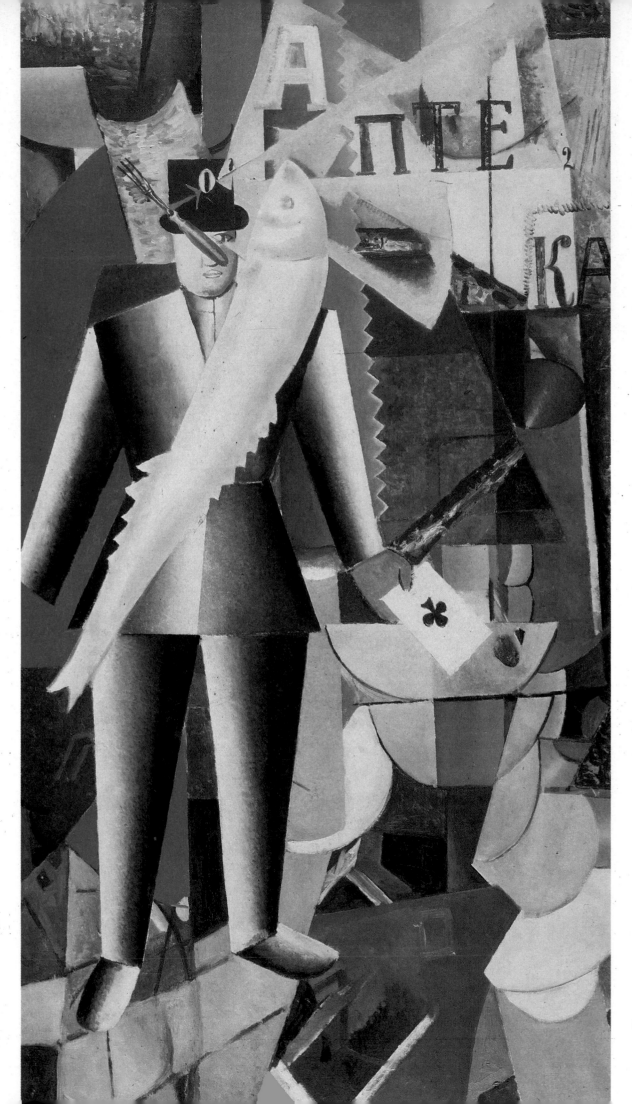

58

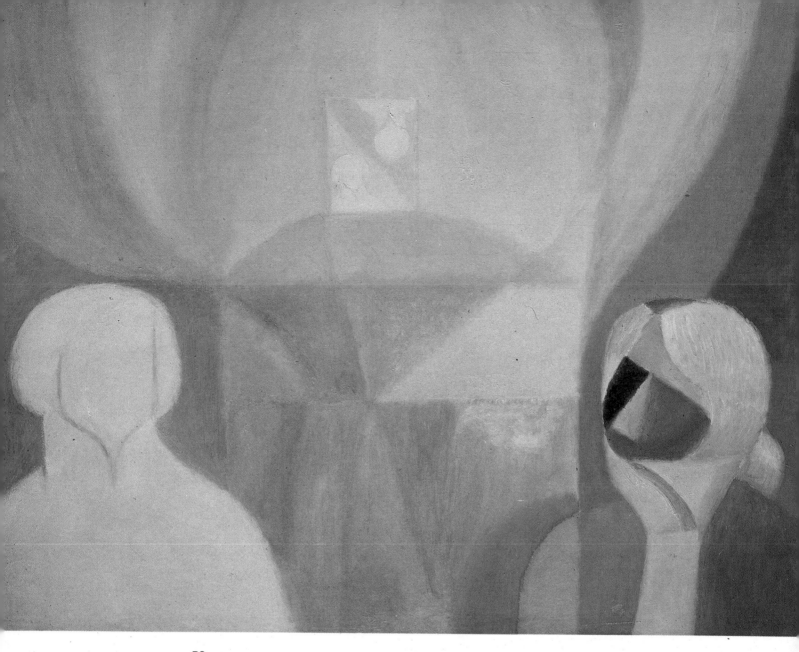

59

**58  Kasimir Malevich.** 1878—1935
AVIATOR. 1914
Oil on canvas. 124×64 cm
The Russian Museum, Leningrad

**59  Vladimir Sterligov.** 1904—1973
CONVERSATION: QUESTION —
ANSWER. 1963
Oil on plywood. 67.5×87 cm
Private collection, Leningrad

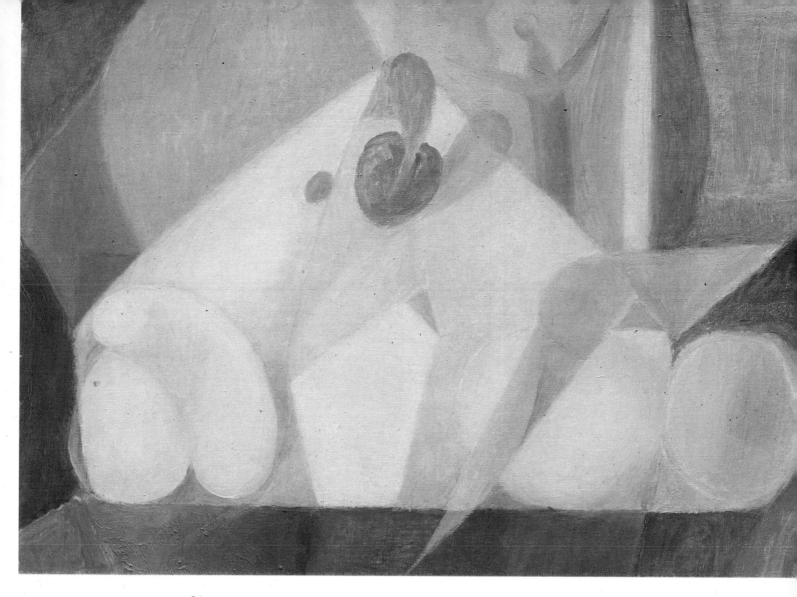

61

**60  Vladimir Sterligov.** 1904—1973
EQUILIBRIUM. 1928
Oil on panel. 23.5×17.5 cm
Private collection, Leningrad

**61  Vladimir Sterligov.** 1904—1973
SURROUNDING GEOMETRY. 1963
Oil on panel. 33×44 cm
Private collection, Leningrad

62

62  **Pavel Filonov.** 1883—1941
COW-TENDERS. 1914
Oil on canvas. 117✕152.5 cm
The Russian Museum, Leningrad

63  **Pavel Filonov.** 1883—1941
PEASANT FAMILY. 1915
Oil on canvas. 89✕72 cm
The Russian Museum, Leningrad

64

**64** **Tatyana Glebova.** 1900—1985
ANIMALS. 1930
Oil on canvas. 81×92 cm
Private collection, Leningrad

**65** **Tatyana Glebova.** 1900—1985
DEAD BIRD. 1937. Detail
Oil on canvas. 33.5×38 cm
Private collection, Leningrad

67

**66   Tatyana Glebova.** 1900—1985
THE LAST COMPOSITION. 1985
Crayons. 42×30 cm
Private collection, Leningrad

**67   Kasimir Malevich.** 1878—1935
TOWN
Gouache and white and Chinese ink on
coloured paper pasted on cardboard.
17.5×17 cm
The A. Radishchev Art Museum, Saratov

68

**68   Vera Yermolayeva.** 1893—1938
THREE FIGURES. 1928. Detail
Watercolours and gouache. 33×34 cm
The Russian Museum, Leningrad

69

**69   Vera Yermolayeva.** 1893—1938
A HOUSE AND A HORSE. 1928. Detail
Gouache. 20×21.2 cm
The Russian Museum, Leningrad

**70  Vasily Chekrygin.** 1897—1922
FATE. 1922
Oil on canvas. 143×107.5 cm
The Russian Museum, Leningrad

**71  Vasily Chekrygin.** 1897—1922
OLD MAN BLESSING THE ANIMALS.
Illustration for the book *Me!*
by V. Mayakovsky. 1913
Lithograph. 19×15.3 cm
The Russian Museum, Leningrad

72

74  **Vera Yermolayeva.** 1893—1938
LUCRETIUS POINTING AT THE SUN.
Based on the poem *De rerum natura*
by Titus Lucretius Carus. 1934
Gouache. 32×21.6 cm
The Russian Museum, Leningrad

72  **Vasily Chekrygin.** 1897—1922
COMPOSITION. 1922
Charcoal. 23.8×27.1 cm
The Russian Museum, Leningrad

75  **Kliment Redko.** 1897—1925
IN THE LAND OF MURMAN. 1925
Oil on canvas. 107×80.5 cm
The Russian Museum, Leningrad

73  **Kuzma Petrov-Vodkin.** 1878—1939
AFTER THE BATTLE. 1923
Oil on canvas. 154×121.5 cm
The Central Army Museum, Moscow

76  **Pavel Kondratyev.** 1902—1985
ANGEL. 1985
Watercolours and gouache. 30×40 cm
Private collection, Leningrad

77

**77 Pavel Kondratyev.** 1902—1985
OVER THE DITCHES. From the *Nurses*
series. 1983
Crayons. 29.5×39 cm
Private collection, Leningrad

78

78 **Pavel Basmanov.** Born 1906
A STROLL WITH THE CHILDREN. 1931
Watercolours. 14.5×18.2 cm
The Russian Museum, Leningrad

79 **Mikhail Matiushin.** 1861—1934
MOVEMENT IN SPACE. 1918
Oil on canvas. 124×168 cm
The Russian Museum, Leningrad

On the fly-leaf:

**Konstantin Yuon.** 1875—1958
**REALM OF PLANETS.** From *The Creation* series.
1908—09
Indian ink and lead pencil. 51×66.9 cm
The Russian Museum, Leningrad

On the cover:

**Kliment Redko.** 1897—1925
MIDNIGHT SUN (AURORA BOREALIS). 1925
Oil on canvas. 107×80.5 cm
The Russian Museum, Leningrad

ФАНТАСТИЧЕСКИЕ СЮЖЕТЫ
В ТВОРЧЕСТВЕ
РУССКИХ ХУДОЖНИКОВ

*Альбом (на английском языке)*

Издательство „Аврора". Ленинград, 1989

Изд. № 1559. (7-50)

ЛПО „Типография имени Ивана Федорова"
Printed and bound in the USSR